Rotten School Day

Felice Arena and Phil Kettle

illustrated by
Mitch Vane

RISING ★ STARS

First published in Great Britain by
RISING STARS UK LTD 2005
76 Farnaby Road, Bromley, BR1 4BH

For information visit our website at:
www.risingstars-uk.com

British Library Cataloguing in Publication Data

A CIP record for this book is available from the British Library.

ISBN: 1-905056-12-5

First published in 2004 by
MACMILLAN EDUCATION AUSTRALIA PTY LTD
627 Chapel Street, South Yarra, Australia 3141

Visit our website at www.macmillan.com.au

Associated companies and representatives throughout the world.

Project Management by Limelight Press Pty Ltd
Cover and text design by Lore Foye
Illustrations by Mitch Vane

Printed and bound in Great Britain by
Mackays of Chatham plc, Chatham, Kent

Contents

Nick   *Matt*

CHAPTER 1

Gross Girls

Best friends Nick and Matt sit next to each other in class. They are whispering together, trying to ignore the two girls who are sitting directly behind them.

Nick "Why do they have to giggle like that?"

Matt "I know, it's a pain. Hey! One of them just hit me on the head with a scrunched up piece of paper."

Nick "We should get them back!"

Matt "You sure you want to do that?"

Nick "What? What do you mean?"

Matt "I think they like you."

Nick "What? Err, gross!"

Matt "I know. But look, see how they're staring at you. If you try to get them back they'll think you like them. They'll probably want to kiss you!"

Nick "No way! I'd get girl germs!"
Matt "Yes, big time!"

Suddenly Nick and Matt's teacher, Mrs. Binkle, warns them to stop talking and to do their school work, or else. The girls giggle again.

Matt "I can't believe that! Your girlfriends got us into trouble."

Nick "They're *not* my girlfriends. Hey—they just hit me on the head ... with a rubber!"

Matt "And they got me again, too!"

Nick "That does it. Let's get them back!"

Nick and Matt scrunch up some
paper balls and throw them back
at the girls—just as Mrs. Binkle
turns from the blackboard, towards
the class.

CHAPTER 2

A Date with the Blackboard

Nick and Matt try to explain to Mrs. Binkle that it wasn't their fault. But she's not in the mood for excuses.

She punishes the boys by making them stay in during playtime and write on the board twenty times: "We must never throw things in class".

Nick "Did you see the girls' faces when we got caught?"

Matt "Yes, they couldn't stop laughing."

Nick "Girls are freaks!"

Matt "Well, not all of them."

Nick "Yes, they are!"

Matt "My mum's not a freak."

Nick "Okay, mums and
grandmothers don't count because
they're cool. But all other girls are!"

Matt "What about that singer
you like?"

Nick "Okay, mums, grandmothers
and cool singers don't count."

Matt "And what about our football coach, Miss Bruno. She's pretty good."

Nick "Okay! Okay! Mums, grandmothers, pop singers and Miss Bruno don't count."

Matt "And what about ... "

Nick "Matt! Stop! Forget it. Have you nearly finished?"

Matt "Yes, just one more line
to write."

Nick "Me too. But for the last one
I'm going to write: 'Girls are really
gross, especially Mrs. Binkle'."

Matt "You can't do that. She'll see
it and then we'll be in really
big trouble."

Nick "Don't worry, I'll rub it out before she gets back!"

Matt "Cool. Then I'm going to write: 'The girls should be doing this, not us'."

Nick "Nice one!"

Seconds later, Mrs. Binkle suddenly appears.

CHAPTER 3

Top Gun Duty

Nick and Matt are sent to Mr. Blake's office—Mr. Blake is the head teacher. They are told to return at lunchtime, eat their lunch with him, then do photocopying duties.

Nick "How many sheets did
Mr. Blake say we have to copy?"

Matt "A hundred."

Nick "And how many have we done
so far?"

Matt "Only ten. You and your dumb
idea to write that message on
the board."

Nick "You wrote one, too!"

Matt "Only because you did it."

The photocopying machine coughs and splutters.

Nick "What's happening? Something's wrong with it."

Matt "Should I go and get Mr. Blake from the staff room?"

Nick "No, just hit it on the side. That's what my dad does when he tries to get a better picture on our old telly."

Matt whacks the photocopying machine with his fist. A few moments later it begins to groan loudly and then out of the blue, it uncontrollably spits out sheets of paper all over the office.

Nick "What have you done?"

Matt "What have I done? It was your stupid idea to hit it!"

Nick "We've got to stop it somehow. Before Mr. Blake gets back! It's going berserk!"

As the boys struggle to stop the machine, the head teacher suddenly returns.

CHAPTER 4

A Ball of Trouble

Mr. Blake is so upset with Nick and Matt that after lunch he doesn't allow them to play rounders with their class. Instead, they are made to pick up litter from the playground.

Nick "You know it wasn't our fault. Nothing really has been our fault today. We're victims."

Matt "We're what?"

Nick "Victims. I heard it on a TV show last night. If we had a lawyer we'd have a pretty good case."

Matt "A suitcase?"

Nick "No, bird brain, a *case*. A good reason why we shouldn't have got in trouble in the first place."

Matt "Yes, you're right. Dumb girls getting us into trouble! They should be the ones picking up litter. Look at them over there. They're laughing at us."

As the boys glare at the girls, one of their classmates hits the ball in the direction of the boys. The ball lands right by their feet. Nick and Matt dive for it.

Nick "It's mine!"

Matt "No, it's mine! I can throw better than you."

Nick "No, you can't."

The boys wrestle for the ball until eventually Nick breaks away with it.

Matt "Nick, let me do it—you're a hopeless thrower!"

Nick ignores Matt and tosses the ball with all his might. The ball whizzes over the top of Nick and Matt's classmates and straight through the library window—*crash*!!!

CHAPTER 5

How Bad Can It Get?

Nick and Matt get an ear-bashing from the head ... again. They are told to sit still in his office and not to move a muscle until the home-time bell rings. When it does, Mr. Blake then tells the boys to think about their day and to come in with a better attitude tomorrow. Nick and Matt walk across the playground, glad to be going home.

Nick "I can't wait to get out of here!"

Matt "You can say that again!"

Nick "How unlucky were we today?"

Matt "Yes!"

Nick "Well, at least it can't get any worse."

Matt "Um, maybe it can. Look!"

Nick follows Matt's stare to see
that he's spotted the two girls that
got them into trouble earlier in the
day. The girls approach the boys and
hand Nick a note. They run off,
giggling loudly. Nick reads the note.

Nick "Err gross! Haven't we suffered enough!"

Matt snatches the note from Nick's hand and reads:
"We think you guys are really cute. We can't wait to see you both tomorrow.
Lots of hugs and kisses,
Joanna and Belinda xoxo"

Matt "Whoa! You're right, that's bad!"

Nick "You can say that again. This has been the worst school day ever. Bring on tomorrow!"

BOYS RULE!

School Lingo

Nick *Matt*

board A board in the classroom is used by the teacher (and sometimes picked-on pupils!) to do demonstrations. It can be an electronic white board.

class clown A pupil who likes to do funny things to make his or her classmates laugh. The class clown isn't usually very popular with the teacher.

head teacher The head of the school, the person with all the power.

homework Schoolwork that pupils have to complete at home (and it's usually really boring!).

teacher's pet The teacher's favourite pupil—two-legged, not four—usually someone who loves to suck up to the teacher.

33

BOYS RULE!
School Must-dos

☞ Never forget to eat your lunch. It's hard to think without food in your stomach.

☞ Be kind to your teachers. Can you imagine what it would be like if you had to look after 30 versions of you?

☞ Remember to put your name on everything—pencil case, uniform, bag and books. You never know when you might lose them.

☞ Remember not to leave any food like fruit in the bottom of your bag or desk—it will turn really gross and make all your books stink.

☞ Don't ever be afraid to tell someone if another kid is giving you a hard time. No-one likes a bully.

☞ Use the playground—not the classroom—to kick a football. You can kick it further outside!

☞ Always listen carefully when the teacher is speaking—you don't want to miss out on learning something great (or have to write lines on the board during playtime).

School Instant Info

The country that has the most primary schools is China. They have more than 800 000.

The head teacher in the TV series "The Simpsons" is called Principal Skinner.

In 2002, primary schools in Melbourne, Australia, built the longest Lego structure ever! It was in the shape of a millipede and it measured 1014.8 metres long.

The world's largest school is the City Montessori School in India. It has over 26 000 students!

In the enormously popular Harry Potter book series, Harry attends Hogwarts—the best wizard school in the land.

School pupils in the USA and in Britain begin their school year in September. Pupils in Australia begin their school year in January.

Primary schools are called elementary schools in the USA.

Think Tank

1 Who or what is a head teacher?

2 What does 2 + 2 + 2 + 11 − 3 equal?

3 What do you carry your schoolbooks in?

4 Where do you keep all your pencils?

5 What is an electronic white board?

6 Name two days of the week most pupils don't go to school?

7 What's homework?

8 What's the place at school called where you can eat food?

Answers

1 The head teacher is the person who is head of the school.

2 $2+2+11-3=14$

3 You carry your books in your school bag.

4 You keep all your pencils in a pencil case.

5 An electronic board used for demonstrations.

6 Most pupils don't go to school on Saturday or Sunday.

7 Homework is schoolwork that you do at home.

8 The canteen is where you can eat food at school.

How did you score?

- If you got all 8 answers correct, then you deserve an A+! You love school and you love to learn.

- If you got 6 answers correct, you also enjoy learning new things and always love a challenge.

- If you got fewer than 4 answers correct, then you like school, sort of, but can get easily distracted sometimes. You also know that when you focus you can be the best pupil ever!

Felice → ← Phil

Hi Guys!

We have heaps of fun reading and want you to, too. We both believe that being a good reader is really important and so cool.

Try out our suggestions to help you have fun as you read.

At school, why don't you use "Rotten School Day" as a play and you and your friends can be the actors. Set the scene for your play. You won't need to bring in too many props as there are plenty around at school every day for this one! Just use your imagination to create the broken window.

So ... have you decided who is going to be Nick and who is going to be Matt? Now, with your friends, read and act out our story in front of the class.

We have a lot of fun when we go to schools and read our stories. After we finish the kids all clap really loudly. When you've finished your play your classmates will do the same. Just remember to look out the window—there might be a talent scout from a television station watching you!

Reading at home is really important and a lot of fun as well.

Take our books home and get someone in your family to read them with you. Maybe they can take on a part in the story.

Remember, reading is a whole lot of fun.

So, as the frog in the local pond would say, Read-it!

And remember, Boys Rule!

BOYS RULE!

When We Were Kids

Felice

Phil

Felice "What was your favourite subject at school? Was it sport?"

Phil "Nope."

Felice "History?"

Phil "Nope."

Felice "Maths?"

Phil "Nope."

Felice "Music? Science? Art?"

Phil "Nope, nope and kind of!"

Felice "I give up! What was it?"

Phil "Lunchtime, where I learned all I need to know about the art of eating!"

BOYS RULE!

What a Laugh!

Q Why did the schoolboy take a ladder to school?

A Because it was a high school.

BOYS RULE!

Gone Fishing	The Tree House	Golf Legends	Camping Out	Bike Daredevils
Water Rats	Skateboard Dudes	Tennis Ace	Basketball Buddies	Secret Agent Heroes
Wet World	Rock Star	Pirate Attack	Olympic Champions	Race Car Dreamers
Hit the Beach	Rotten School Day	Halloween Gotcha!	Battle of the Games	On the Farm

44

BOYS RULE! books are available from most booksellers.
For mail order information please call Rising Stars
on 01933 443862 or visit www.risingstars-uk.com